THE ARTICULATE CHILD

*40 Thought-Provoking Mathematical Questions
to Mentally Stimulate Your Child*

Patrick I. Ezeadikwa

The Articulate Child

Copyright © 2025 by Patrick I. Ezeadikwa

All rights reserved.

No portion of this book may be reproduced in any form without written permission from the publisher or author, except as permitted by U.S. copyright law.

CONTENTS

Q. 1	1
Q. 2	5
Q. 3	9
Q. 4	13
Q. 5	17
Q. 6	21
Q. 7	25
Q. 8	29
Q. 9	33
Q. 10	37
Q. 11	41
Q. 12	45
Q. 13	49
Q. 14	53
Q. 15	57
Q. 16	61
Q. 17	65
Q. 18	69
Q. 19	73
Q. 20	77
Q. 21	81
Q. 22	85
Q. 23	89
Q. 24	93
Q. 25	97

CONTENTS

Q. 26	101
Q. 27	105
Q. 28	109
Q. 29	113
Q. 30	117
Q. 31	121
Q. 32	125
Q. 33	129
Q. 34	133
Q. 35	137
Q. 36	141
Q. 37	145
Q. 38	149
Q. 39	153
Q. 40	157

The Articulate Child

The Articulate Child

Q. 1

You threw a ball straight up from your hand and it landed back on your hand. From the moment the ball left your hand to the moment just before it landed on your hand, did the ball ever come to a stop?

The Articulate Child

Answer

Yes, the ball came to a momentary stop. The ball came to a stop when it reached the peak of its upward motion before it began to come down.

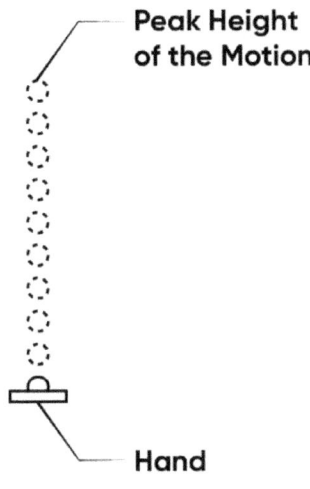

The Articulate Child

Q. 2

When a pendulum is in motion, does the ball ever come to a stop?

The Articulate Child

Answer

Yes. The pendulum comes to a stop at the moment it changes direction at points A and E.

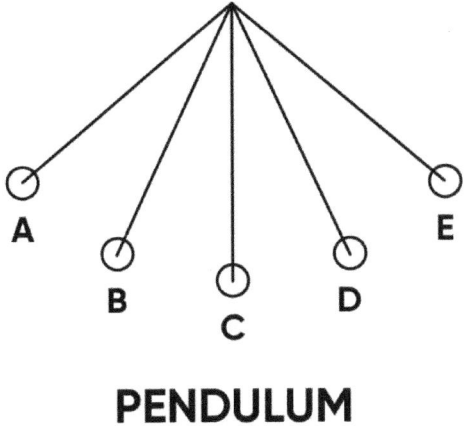

PENDULUM

The Articulate Child

Q. 3

A baseball pitcher throws a baseball to a batter. When the batter hits the ball, does the ball momentarily stop its motion?

The Articulate Child

Answer

Yes. The ball comes to a stop when it makes contact with the bat.

The Articulate Child

Q. 4

There are 2 water faucets with running water at a constant speed. You placed 1 cup under each faucet. Cup A was placed 2 feet under the faucet while Cup B was placed 2.5 feet under the faucet. Which cup will fill up faster?

The Articulate Child

Answer

Cup A will fill up faster because it's closer to the faucet. (Speed = Distance per Time). Since the speed is constant for both faucets, the farther the cup is from the faucet, the longer it will take for the cup to fill up.

The Articulate Child

Q. 5

You're sitting on a 4-legged chair. You weigh 100 pounds. Ignore the weight of the chair. Assume your weight is evenly distributed on the chair. How much weight does one leg of the chair carry?

The Articulate Child

Answer

Each leg will carry ¼ (a quarter) of 100 LBS = 25 LBS.

The Articulate Child

Q. 6

You have a wooden triangle and a rectangle. The triangle area is 10 square feet, and the rectangle area is 10 square feet. If a constant force of air is blowing at both shapes, which shape will experience the most pressure?

> # The Articulate Child

Answer

Both shapes will experience the same amount of pressure because they have the same area and the air force is constant. (Pressure = Force per Area).

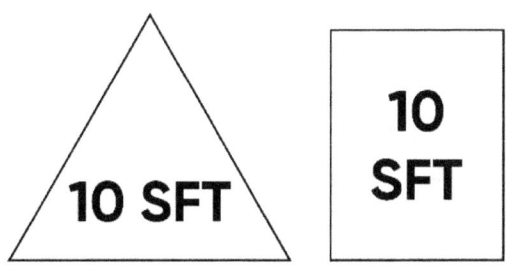

The Articulate Child

Q. 7

Two sprinters who are capable of running at the same speed are about to compete. Sprinter A wore tightly fitted clothes while Sprinter B wore loosely fitted clothes. Who would probably finish first?

The Articulate Child

Answer

Sprinter A will most probably finish first because he/she won't experience backward air drag since his/her clothes are tightly fitted.

The Articulate Child

Q. 8

You have 2 sieves, Sieve A and Sieve B. Sieve A has 4 equal openings. Sieve B has 20 equal openings. If I pour the same amount of water through both Sieves and the water drains in the same amount of time, what can you conclude about the openings of both Sieves?

The Articulate Child

Answer

Both sieves' openings are of the same area. That's why water drained in both sieves in the same amount of time.

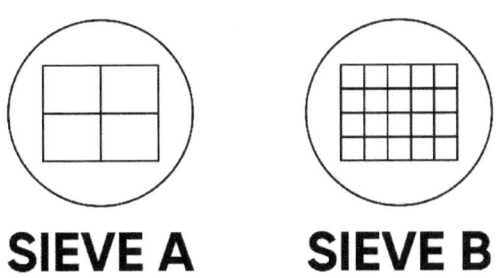

SIEVE A **SIEVE B**

The Articulate Child

Q. 9

You have a rectangular wooden plank 20 feet by 2 feet, which weighs 5 pounds. You oriented the Plank horizontally and placed a 50 pounds metal weight in the middle of the plank. What's the minimum (whole number) force capable of moving the plank and metal weight together? Ignore every environmental and external factor.

The Articulate Child

Answer

A force greater than the sum of 5 LBS and 50 LBS ((5+50) LBS = 55 LBS) will move the setup. Therefore, the minimum whole-number force is 56 lbs.

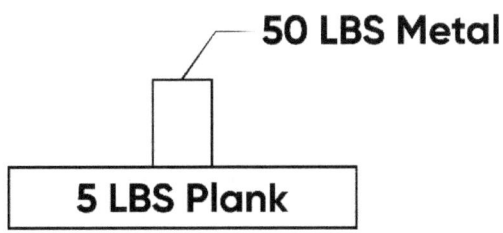

The Articulate Child

Q. 10

You boiled 3 pounds of rice. As soon as the water in the pot dries up, does the rice in the pot weigh more or less than 3 pounds?

The Articulate Child

Answer

The rice grains weigh more because they absorbed a lot of the water while some of the water evaporated.

The Articulate Child

Q. 11

You placed a 50 pounds weight on a wooden stool, and the stool didn't break. You placed a 100 pounds weight on the same wooden stool and the stool broke. What's the maximum weight the stool can carry?

The Articulate Child

Answer

The maximum weight is greater than or equal to 50 pounds but less than 100 pounds.

The Articulate Child

Q. 12

A circular table is 7 feet wide and a square table is 7 feet wide. Which of these tables have more surface space?

The Articulate Child

Answer

The square table is more spacious. Area of circle is 3.14 x (3.5 feet)^2 = 38.4 ft². Area of square is 7 feet * 7 feet = 49 ft².

The Articulate Child

Q. 13

For a circular table with 3 legs to stand the most stable, at what angle should the legs be spaced between one another?

The Articulate Child

Answer

The 3 legs should be spaced at 120 degrees from one another. (360 degrees / 3 legs).

The Articulate Child

Q. 14

When you stand for a long time, what would cause your legs to fatigue? Ignore every external factor.

The Articulate Child

Answer

The weight of your body will cause your legs to fatigue.

The Articulate Child

Q. 15

You're standing in front of 2 walls, Wall A and Wall B. Wall A is sloped at an upgrade and makes a 15-degree angle from you. Wall B is also sloped at an upgrade and makes a 75-degree angle from you. Which wall is easier to climb?

The Articulate Child

Answer

Wall B will be easier to climb because it's less steep compared to Wall A.

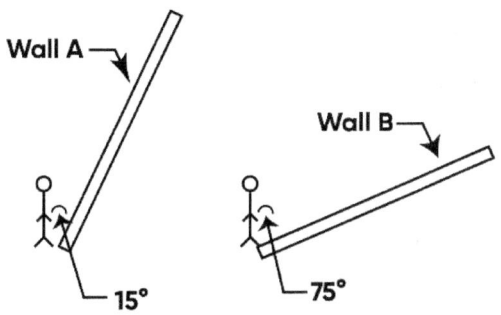

The Articulate Child

Q. 16

You're riding your bicycle on a flat roadway and you're peddling at a constant rate. Your bicycle is moving at a speed of 20 mph. When you get into a downgraded portion of the road and you're still peddling at a constant rate, will your bicycle speed remain the same?

The Articulate Child

Answer

The speed of the bicycle will increase because gravity is pushing down on you and the bicycle.

The Articulate Child

Q. 17

There are 2 cylinders, Cylinder A and Cylinder B. Both cylinders weigh the same and have the same diameter. Cylinder A is 10 feet long and Cylinder B is 5 feet long. Both cylinders are rolling in the direction of the wind. Which of the cylinders will roll faster?

The Articulate Child

Answer

Cylinder B will feel the most pressure because its surface area is smaller than that of cylinder A.

The Articulate Child

Q. 18

A refrigerator is 2 feet wide, 7 feet high, and 1 inch wall thickness. If a 2 feet by 2 feet pizza box is oriented horizontally, can it fit inside the refrigerator?

The Articulate Child

Answer

It won't fit inside the refrigerator because the inside width of the fridge is less than 2 feet.

The Articulate Child

Q. 19

There is a 20-feet-long wooden plank. This plank weighs 30 pounds. A 2 inch metal cube is placed under the plank at one end, and a 3 inch plastic cube is placed under the other end of the plank. Which of the cubes carries more weight?

The Articulate Child

Answer

Both cubes will carry the same amount of weight of the wooden plank (30 LBS / 2 cubes = 15 LBS per cube) because the cube size doesn't matter.

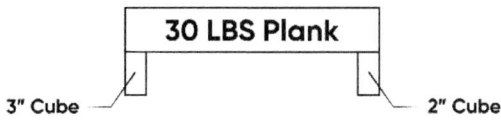

The Articulate Child

Q. 20

There are two plastic boxes. Box A weighs 10 pounds and Box B weighs 5 pounds. You placed the 10 pounds box on a smooth flat surface and applied a 35 pounds force. You placed the 5 pounds box on a fairly rough flat surface and applied a 50 pounds force. Which of the boxes will most likely move the farthest after it comes to a stop?

The Articulate Child

Answer

Box A will move the farthest because there's no friction on its surface to eventually stop its motion.

The Articulate Child

Q. 21

The maximum weight limit of a rope is 60 pounds. If you hang a weight of 60 pounds on the rope and there's 4 inches of thick snow residue on the weight, will the rope break?

The Articulate Child

Answer

Yes. The rope will most probably break because the snow residue has weight.

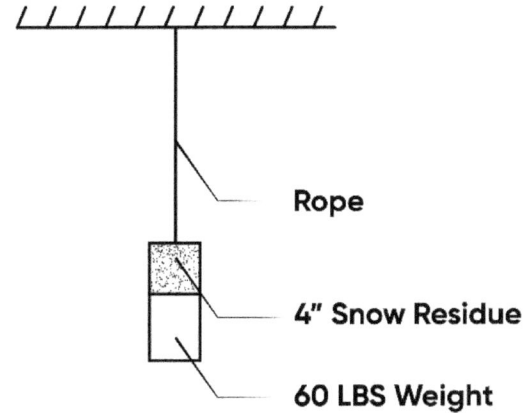

The Articulate Child

Q. 22

One end of a 3-feet rope is tied to a ceiling while the other end of the rope is tied to a 10 pounds concrete block. The concrete block is hanging from the ceiling. What point on the rope feels the tension from the hanging block?

The Articulate Child

Answer

The whole length of the rope feels the tension. (Isaac Newton's Third Law: for every action there is an equal and opposite reaction). While 10 pounds of concrete is pulling on the rope in a downward direction, the ceiling is holding up the rope with 10 pounds of force in the upward direction.

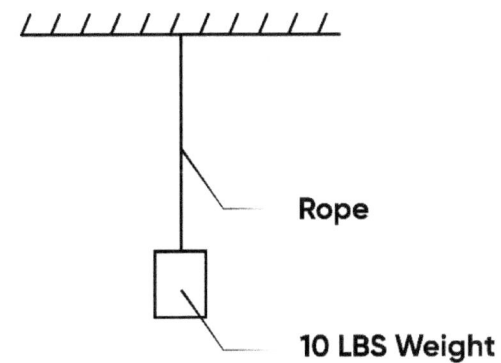

The Articulate Child

Q. 23

You have several bookshelves. Each bookshelf is 5 feet wide and 1 foot high and weighs 3 pounds. The maximum weight each shelf can carry is 8 pounds. You stack 3 bookshelves; will the shelves stand? If not, which shelf will break?

The Articulate Child

Answer

The shelves will stand. The bottom shelf is carrying a total of 6 pounds from the 2 shelves above it. The middle shelf is carrying a total of 3 pounds from the 1 shelf above it.

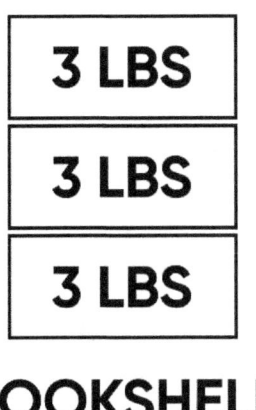

The Articulate Child

Q. 24

You tossed a tennis Ball A 7 feet high to serve and the ball landed on the opposite side of the court at a particular point. You stood at the initial serving spot, tossed a tennis Ball B 8 feet high and served. It landed at the same spot as the initial ball. Did any of the balls travel farther?

The Articulate Child

Answer

Ball B traveled farther than Ball A. As the opposite or adjacent side increases, hypotenuse increases.

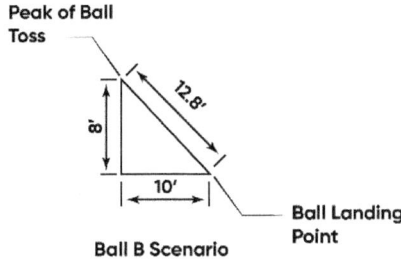

Ball B Scenario

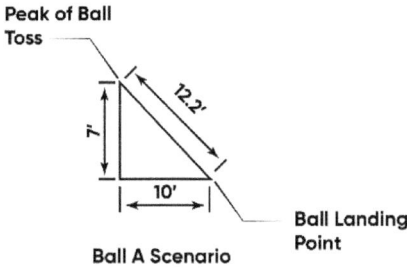

Ball A Scenario

… The Articulate Child

Q. 25

The series of Step A is 20 feet long and each step is 0.5 foot high and 1 foot deep. Another series of Step B is 30 feet long and each step is 0.25 foot high and 1 foot deep. Which series of steps is easier to climb?

ns to the way forward I wish to take, in trying to link the literary or aesthetic world of children's literature with our adult experience of childhood. Part Two, therefore, will make use of the works of several philosophers of what I should call broadly 'sensibility', including Emmanuel Levinas, Martha Nussbaum, Stanley Cavell and Cora Diamond, whose concern for ethical questions is intimately connected with their sense of such questions' embeddedness in everyday, natural human life, and in the culture, pre-eminently literary, which is generated by our natural life and which feeds back into it. My approach to philosophical questions about children's literature will continue, as in Part One, to use particular literary texts as 'case studies'; but the main consideration will be the nature of the exchange between 'adult' and 'child' in the actual reading of such texts, between the implied adult narrator or narrators and the implied child reader - all of which must be, in the nature of the case, also realized within the mind of the actual adult reader reading to or being read by the actual child. Is there, as it were, an 'adult' way of attending to children's literature which does not betray the fundamental relationship of equality, of a shared world, which it both rests on and promotes? Is there a way of seeing the 'child' and the 'adult' as aspects of our being, which can be held in creative balance in our actual exchanges with real children, and in our reading with them or to them - with all the complex and ambiguous power-relations and negotiations of identity that these exchanges will always involve? And what does all this mean for the ways in which we might properly 'criticize', in a philosophically respectable way, the books we read with children, or which children read themselves?

The Articulate Child

Answer

Step B is easier to climb because it's less steep compared to Step A. Step A slope is 50% (0.5 FT / 1 FT = 0.5). Step B slope is 25% (0.25 FT / 1 FT = 0.25).

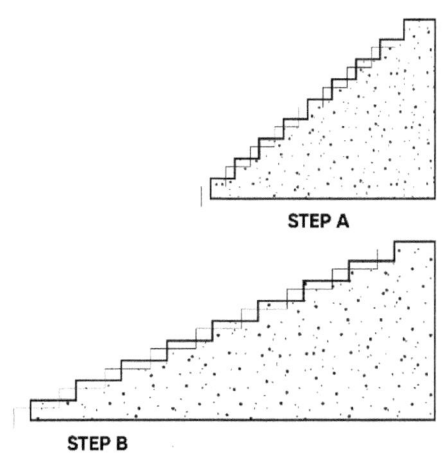

The Articulate Child

Q. 26

There are 9 bricks, each of which weighs 3 pounds. These bricks are arranged in 3 rows and 3 columns. If you throw a 5 pounds sandbag at the bricks, the sandbag is capable of knocking down the brick. Which of the bricks will be easiest and most challenging to knock down?

The Articulate Child

Answer

a. The bricks that are easiest to knock down are the top outside bricks (1 & 3) because they have less restriction from other bricks, while other bricks have more restriction from more bricks.

b. The hardest brick to knock down is the middle bottom brick (8) because it has restrictions from all sides.

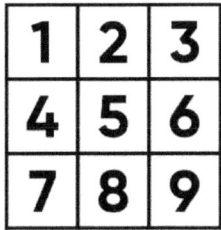

9 BRICKS

The Articulate Child

Q. 27

You weigh 160 pounds. Will it be easier to lift a 40 pounds weight from the ground or catch a falling 40 pounds weight?

The Articulate Child

Answer

It will be easier to lift the 40 pounds weight from the ground while it is at rest. The falling 40 pounds weight will require more effort to stop the motion and hold onto it.

The Articulate Child

Q. 28

There is a 4-legged stool. The maximum weight limit of each leg is 100 pounds. If you place a 401 pounds weight at the center of this stool, will the stool hold up?

The Articulate Child

Answer

Each leg will carry 100.25 (401 LBS / 4 Legs = 100.25 LBS/Leg). This exceeds the weight limit of each leg.

The Articulate Child

Q. 29

There is a circular fire pit. The inside radius is 1 foot. The outside radius is 6 feet. There is a long, 1-foot-diameter rubber pipe. How many times will the rubber pipe wrap around the fire pit between the inside and outside of the radii?

The Articulate Child

Answer

The rubber pipe will wrap around 5 times. The difference in radius is 5 feet. The diameter of the rubber pipe is 1 foot. 5 x 1 foot diameter pipe = 5 - 1 foot diameter pipe.

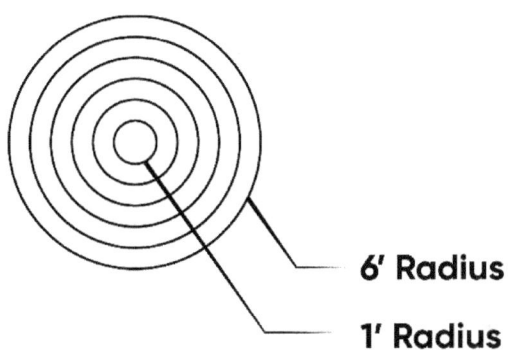

6' Radius

1' Radius

The Articulate Child

Q. 30

A ball weighs 10 pounds. The ball is tied to a rope. The rope is tied to a nail. The nail is punched into a wall. Between the nail, the rope, and the wall, which one is carrying the most weight of the ball? Which one is carrying the most weight?

The Articulate Child

Answer

a. The nail, rope, and wall are carrying the same amount of ball weight.

b. The wall carries most of the weight because the rope and nail weights are also carried by the wall.

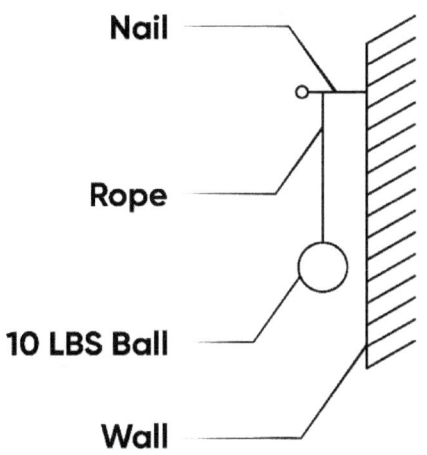

The Articulate Child

Q. 31

I have 2 rectangles of the same size. Rectangle A was cut diagonally. Rectangle B was cut through the middle. Do the 2 cut-outs have the same or different areas?

The Articulate Child

Answer

Both cut-outs have the same area. The original sizes were cut in half, so the final area of the cut-outs is half the original area.

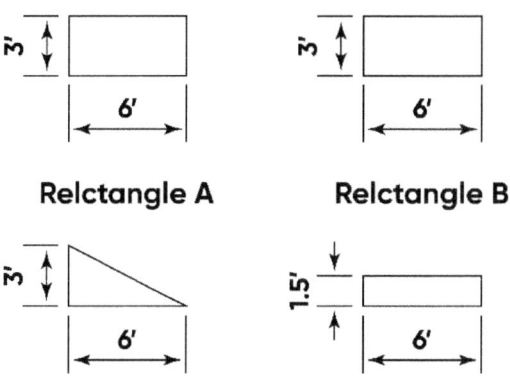

The Articulate Child

Q. 32

I have 3 metal gears (Gear A, Gear B, Gear C) joined side by side. When Gear A rotates counterclockwise, in what direction will Gears B and C rotate?

The Articulate Child

Answer

Gear B will rotate clockwise while Gear C will rotate counterclockwise.

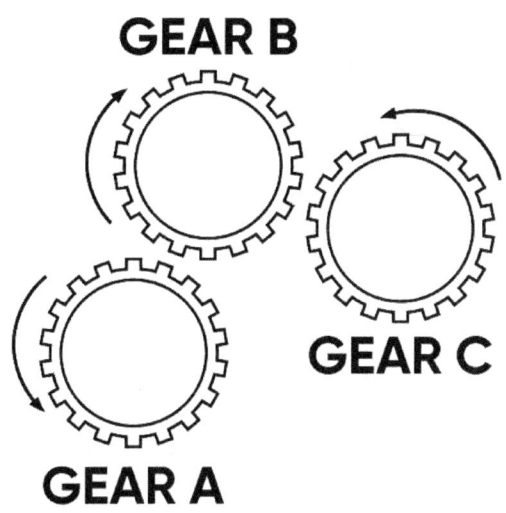

The Articulate Child

Q. 33

You have 2 rectangles of the same size, 10 feet by 1 foot. In Scenario A, you placed the rectangles horizontally apart. In Scenario B, you placed the rectangles horizontally next to each other, and the sides touched. Will the perimeter of the rectangles in both scenarios be the same?

The Articulate Child

Answer

No. The perimeter of the rectangles in Scenario B will be smaller than the perimeter in Scenario A. The sides of the rectangles that are touching will be eliminated from the calculation.

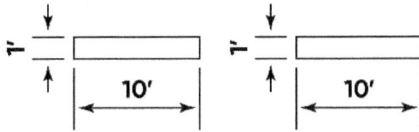

Scenario A

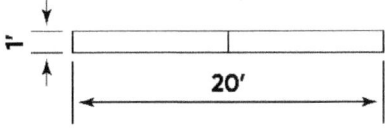

Scenario B

The Articulate Child

Q. 34

You have 2 equilateral triangles and 2 trapezoids. When you fitted all the shapes together, they created a rectangle. Is the sum of the area of the individual shapes same as the rectangle?

The Articulate Child

Answer

Yes. Since the individual shapes make up the whole triangle, the sum of the individual shape areas will equal the area of the rectangle.

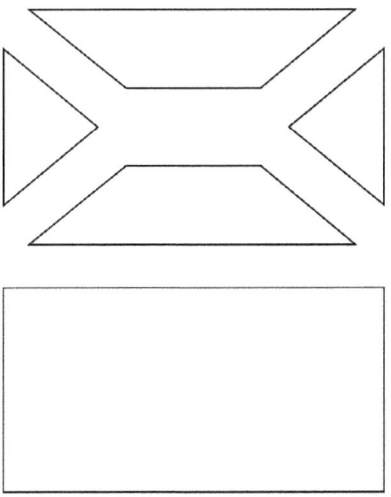

The Articulate Child

Q. 35

A 15 square feet hexagonal tray is carrying 10 cans of soda that weigh 7 pounds total. Another 15 square feet circular tray is carrying 5 cans of soda that weigh 7 pounds total. Which tray will be less stressful to carry?

The Articulate Child

Answer

Both trays will feel the same stress because they are subjected to the same weight over the same area. (Stress = Force per Area).

The Articulate Child

Q. 36

There are 2 trucks of equal size. Truck A drives at a maximum speed of 35 mph. Truck B drives at maximum speed of 45 mph. There are 2 different and equal piles of sand to haul from location A to destination B. A trip is completed when a truck goes from location A to destination B. If both trucks are always filled completely for each trip and they drive at the maximum speed, which truck will go on fewer trips?

The Articulate Child

Answer

Regardless of the truck's maximum speed, both trucks will make the same number of trips.

The Articulate Child

Q. 37

There are 2 wooden planks, Plank A and Plank B. Plank A and Plank B are 10 feet long and both weigh 10 pounds. Plank A was laid horizontally on top of 2 – 2 inch cubes placed on both ends. Plank B was placed vertically on top of the middle of Plank A. What should be the minimum weight at each cube?

The Articulate Child

Answer

The total weight of the planks is 20 pounds. Each support will carry half of the total weight, which is 10 pounds.

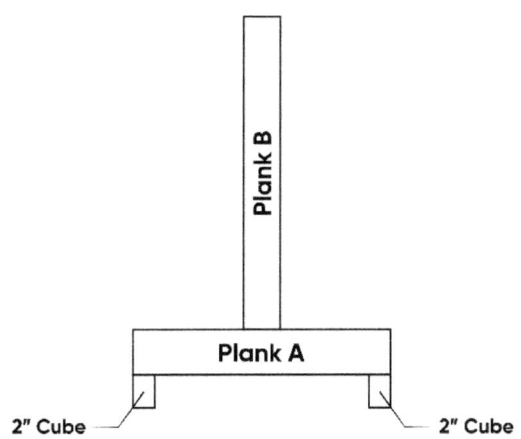

The Articulate Child

Q. 38

You have a cone tank with a volume of 50 cubic feet. There is another rectangular tank with a volume of 50 cubic feet. You have 2 sets of 50 - 1 cubic foot cubes. Will the small cubes completely fit in both tanks?

The Articulate Child

Answer

No. The 50 – 1 cubic foot cubes will fit in the rectangular tank because the cube is the same shape as the rectangle. The 50 – 1 cubic foot cubes will not completely fit in the cone because the cone is a different shape from the cubes. When you put the cubes in the cone tank, there will be many gaps around some of the cubes.

The Articulate Child

Q. 39

You have a foldable wire that is 32 feet long. If you folded the wire into a 4-sided shape, would it be a square or a rectangle?

The Articulate Child

Answer

It will be both a square (32 FT / 4 = 8 FT) and a rectangle (any rectangular dimension, e.g, 10 feet by 6 feet).

The Articulate Child

Q. 40

There is a Pentagon shape. What's the minimum triangle shape that will fill up a Pentagon?

The Articulate Child

Answer

3 triangle shapes will fill up a pentagon shape.

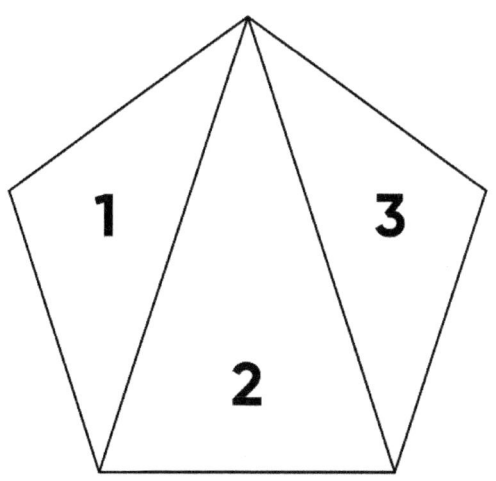

The Articulate Child

www.ingramcontent.com/pod-product-compliance
Lightning Source LLC
LaVergne TN
LVHW081814080526
838199LV00099B/4601